Call Center Humor
The Best of Call Center Management Review

volume 3

Call Center Press
A Division of ICMI, Inc.

Published by:
Call Center Press
A Division of ICMI, Inc.
P.O. Box 6177
Annapolis, Maryland 21401

Copyright 2003 by ICMI, Inc.
First printing, 2001
Second printing, 2003

Printed in the United States of America

ISBN 0-9659093-7-9

*This book is dedicated to my baby daughter, Leah,
and anyone else who drools uncontrollably
and needs to be changed after browsing my column.*

Contents

Foreword

What's so funny about call centers? Well, when you work in a fast-paced, constantly changing industry, you need to be able to see the lighter side of things once in awhile. Call center-related humor obviously touches a chord with managers or we wouldn't have put together a third collection of Greg Levin's "In Your Ear" humor columns.

Greg has been humoring call center managers for years with his quirky, yet on-the-mark satirical insights on industry practices and trends. But, while his viewpoint may be humorous, the topics he touches on are the ones managers struggle with day-in and day-out.

His offbeat perception about common management pains makes this book highly useful. The next time your request for a budget increase gets shot down, agent morale hits an all-time low or your technology initiative goes south — pick it up and give yourself a humor break. I'm sure it will restore your perspective!

Susan Hash, *Editor*
Call Center Management Review

Preface

While it's true that in high school I was voted "Most likely to have a trilogy compendium of call center humor articles published before the age of 33," I never really thought it would happen. And even though my grandfather always used to say, "Keep your nose clean, look both ways before crossing the street, and be either a doctor or somebody who writes nonsensical essays about customer contact," I never really listened. In fact, it really wasn't until I got to college and heard my career counselor say, "Kid, I can see by your grades that you're never going to be a rocket scientist, and certainly not a call center satirist," that I decided what I wanted to be when I grew up.

Since that day, I've dedicated my life to making my classmates and my grandfather proud, and making my college career counselor eat his words. With the publication of this volume that you now hold, I feel that I have achieved all of these goals.

And while I'm not usually one to flaunt his successes, I just wanted to say this to my old career counselor: "I've sold over 16 copies of call center satire books in my career. How many have you sold?"

Greg Levin

Call Center Humor
The Best of Call Center Management Review

volume 3

Customer Service Agents at Singles Bars

Call Center "Personals"

After a day full of forecasting call volumes, organizing training sessions and monitoring agents, a person needs somebody to talk to outside their call center. For many, it's their spouse, significant other — or both. But many call center professionals are single and don't have time to meet people outside of work. While some follow former President Clinton's lead and date people with whom they work, others prefer not to fraternize with their fellow phone folks.

For this reason, I've decided to create a dating service for call center professionals. This will allow them to meet people, outside of their own call center, with whom they share common interests. It will also allow me to raise enough money to have my hair styled properly.

I've already collected several "Call Center Personals" from managers, supervisors and agents looking to score high on the monitoring form of love. (Don't panic if that last sentence made you feel a bit queasy — everybody who proofread this piece had the same reaction.) Here are a few personals to whet your appetite. And please, if you are married or seriously involved with someone, kindly skip to the next chapter — didn't your mother teach you that it is rude to ask for "seconds" before everybody has had "firsts"?

"Dirk" Supervisor

"I'm 6′ 2″ with brown eyes and brown hair, however, with blond hair and blue eyes I'm only 5′ 11″.

Let me warn you, I live on the edge. Yes, I'm a free spirit who's not afraid of adventure, as long as I get senior management's approval first. While I may be wild, I can be as sensitive and caring as the next guy. I enjoy quiet talks about Erlang C and long walks in the call center parking lot on a moonlit night. Call me and I'll take you places, but you'll have to drive as I recently sold my van to help pay for a new IVR system."

"Mona" Call Center Manager

"If you like pina coladas
Or getting caught in the rain,
If you're sick of dumb terminals
That cause real bad eyestrain.
If you like monitoring at midnight
And capturing good calls on tape,
You're the man that I dream of,
Come with me and escape."

"Kevin" Customer Service Agent

"I'm a Romeo rep seeking his Juliet. Oh fair, sweet Juliet, won't thou reveal thyself to me? Let me help thou untangle thy headset cord and be free, free like the birds or the lead agents who no longer have to adhere to schedule. My heart is a queue, a queue filled with love that must be routed to thy workstation.

I beg of thee — oh temptress of the telephone — respond to my call promptly. That will amend what pains me, and help to improve your average speed of answer statistics."

"Connie" Recruiting Director

I spend all day interviewing and testing agent applicants, and now I want somebody to pay attention to me. I'm not looking for much, just somebody with good rapport-building skills, a pleasant voice and the ability to handle multiple tasks at once. At least two years of experience in a monogamous relationship with a call center professional is preferred. Those with less experience but who can cook will be considered. Excellent benefits, including free parking at my apartment and full use of my washer and dryer. Qualified candidates please send cover letter explaining why I should give you the time of day, along with a copy of your dating history and your position on marriage/children. I am an equal opportunity dater, but if you are an outbound telemarketer, you might as well save your stamp.

Separating the Reps from the Replicas

Every call center professional claims that they follow "best practices" when hiring agents, yet their turnover rates remain higher than their body temperature. I think it's time for call center managers to start taking some risks with regard to their hiring procedures. Asking the same tired pre-screening questions — "Why do you want this job?" "What are your strengths and weaknesses?" "You smell great; what's that you're wearing?" — will result in the same tired, rehearsed responses that you've heard from agent applicants for years.

The best way to measure applicants' worth is by catching them off-guard during the interview process. The call center can be a hectic place with crushing call volumes, irate customers and coffee shortages in the break room, so you must seek agents who truly know how to handle unexpected adversity and think on their feet. Below are some suggestions on how to sift out Rambo reps from wimpy replicas during the hiring process.

Place the applicant in a room full of snakes. This will enable you to see how well the applicant responds to extraordinarily stressful situations. Once you've placed the applicant in the snake-infested room, observe his or her behavior through a two-way police mirror. Applicants who merely huddle in the corner and shiver probably aren't the kind of folks who will be able to handle the phones during your peak season. Look for appli-cants who are able to overcome the situation by using their brains. Examples include applicants who get down on the floor and squirm to become "one" with the snakes, and applicants who calmly threaten to sue your company for millions if you don't remove all the serpents immedi-ately. If your call center has a really high-stress environment and you don't feel the snake test is enough, try placing the applicant in a room filled with dentists or Gap salespeople.

Insult the applicant's mother. After going over the applicant's resume and asking some preliminary interview questions, begin casting aspersions about his or her mom. This is a great way to measure how well the applicant will handle abusive customers. Remember, applicants who lose their tempers with you — their possible future boss — are certainly likely to do the same with callers, and thus should be turned away. Applicants who respond to the insults by merely smiling and saying "I agree" probably aren't the best candidates either. Look for applicants who recognize that you've insulted their mothers and who are willing to calmly discuss why you may feel the way you do. Example response: "I'm sorry that you think my mom bears resemblance to a bulldog with leprosy. Maybe if I had some more information I'd understand your point of view."

Tell them they can choose their salary. By giving applicants such freedom, you can measure how responsibly they will handle empowerment. You want agents on whom you can depend to make important decisions with confidence. Applicants who respond to the "salary" question by drooling uncontrollably and yelling out "Papa needs a new pair of shoes!" probably aren't fit to work in a self-directed inbound environment, unless it's that of your rival company. Ideal candidates are those who choose a salary that's within $1,500 of what you have in mind. But don't forget to remind applicants who select salaries within this range that the whole thing was just an exercise and that they will be making $7.50/hour ($7.75 if they have a Master's degree) whether they like it or not.

Check for unusually large or small craniums. This has little to do with the theme of this article, but it's still important. The costs involved in hiring and training new agents are high enough; don't make matters worse by selecting applicants who need custom-fitted headsets. Candidates with craniums smaller than 6″ or larger than that of Jay Leno can cost your company a small fortune and thus should be weeded out during the screening process. But be careful not to put your company at risk for a skull-discrimination lawsuit. For example, it's better to tell a small-headed applicant that he lacks the experience your call center requires than to tell him that you have a policy against hiring people with a grapefruit attached to their neck.

Final Note:

Once you've narrowed the choices down to a few highly qualified agent applicants, make sure that you hire the most annoying ones. The reason for this is that, if they truly are talented, they'll likely soon be stolen from you by another department within your company, and you won't miss them as much if they are irritating.

Questionable Hiring

ha ha ha ha ha ha ha ha ha ha ha ha ha ha ha

Some More Really State-of-the-Art Call Center Technology

In the June 1996 issue of *Call Center Management Review* (then known as *Service Level Newsletter*), I wrote an article for this column titled "Really State-of-the-Art Call Center Technology," which attracted a lot of attention; not because it was particularly insightful or even coherent, but because it was written in beautiful calligraphy and included naked pictures of several ACD vendor spokespeople.

I've since matured as a journalist and feel confident that I can write a "technology" article that draws attention based solely on the quality of the written content. Besides, with the increased competition in the industry, call center vendors have become more conservative, making it extremely difficult to find people at companies like Aspect, Nortel or Avaya willing to pose nude any more.

Here are descriptions of some of the newest and most innovative call center tools. All are still in the final testing stage, and with the exception of one small incident in which a study participant's headset burst into flames, the trials have been successful.

CTI (Comedian-Telephony Integration). Everybody is talking about how call centers have to do more than just satisfy customers — they have to delight them. And what better way is there to delight callers than to make them laugh so hard that they almost throw up right at the beginning of the call? So why not implement the new CTI? Comedian-Telephony Integration — the only call center technology that blends great service with guffaws. As a call arrives, not only does CTI deliver a screen-pop to the agent's PC showing the caller's name and account history, it provides the agent with a photo of the caller and a few customized jokes. Let's say the caller is Mr. Smith, who calls your bank call center every month to verify his account balance. The call might be routed to the agent with the following script: "How ya doing Mr. Smith, if that is, in fact, your real name (pause for chuckle)? I gotta tell you, it's great to be here. Hey, I see your account is really growing — too bad I can't say the same about your hair (pause for a belly laugh)! Maybe you can invest a portion of your dividends in some Rogaine (pause for a chortle)! Nah, I kid you, I'm a kidder. But seriously, how can I help you today, Curly?"

InstaRep. Thanks to the combined efforts of experts in the fields of genetics, microbiology and human resources, call center professionals everywhere have a quick, affordable and effective staffing option that's only a faucet away. The next time your center experiences a sudden call spike, leaving you understaffed and overstressed, grab a packet of InstaRep and just add water. In just minutes you will have a dedicated phone pro ready to tackle virtually any queue. InstaRep — the world's first powdered agent mix approved by the FDA and the FCC — is composed of a complex blend of dehydrated organic molecules and Colombian coffee beans that, when mixed with water, grow rapidly into energetic customer service professionals. Each InstaRep is guaranteed to provide at least three weeks of top-notch service. However, using an InstaRep for more than a month is not recommended, as that is usually the time when they begin complaining about eyestrain and asking for raises. InstaRep comes in "original," or "low fat" for those of you who have particularly small workstations. Warning: Be sure to add the exact amount of water indicated on the packet. Not adding enough water may result in rigid InstaReps that break into pieces whenever schedules change. Adding too much water will cause InstaReps' heads to swell and increase the chances of them being mistaken for marketing managers.

Dreamonitor. Don't have enough time to adequately monitor your agents' calls? Is your staff complaining that they don't receive enough feedback on their performance? Did you forget to turn off your iron this morning? If you answered "yes" to that last one, do what you need to do and come back to this article later. If you answered "yes" to just the first two, have I got a solution for you: Dreamonitor. This groundbreaking technology enables you to listen to taped agent calls at home while sleeping. Dreamonitor's special recording device causes the voices from the taped call to penetrate your brain's memory mode while in the REM stage of sleep. You'll wake up and remember every aspect of each call you heard! The only drawback found during tests of the product occurred when one supervisor's personal dreams interfered with the tape, causing her to think that one of her agents was Antonio Banderas.

Priority Queuing

ha ha ha ha ha ha ha ha ha ha ha ha ha ha

The REAL Impact of Y2K on Call Centers*

This column was originally published in December 1998. Every prediction came true.

Nobody really knows exactly what's going to happen to call centers after the clock strikes midnight on December 31, 1999. Actually, there's a guy named Fred in Iowa who knows, but he's not talking until Bill Gates pays him $5 billion. Everybody is scrambling now to ensure that their call center technology is Y2K compliant and that customers feel secure about the safety of their personal accounts and the company's products, etc. You hear doomsday advisers speak about catastrophic increases in call/email volume, devastating decreases in revenue, and higher levels of hysteria than when Seinfeld went off the air.

But I believe it's the little things call center professionals aren't thinking about that are going to jump up and bite them when 2000 rolls around. Here are a few of the smaller Y2K issues that threaten to cripple your call center and emotional well-being if you don't begin panicking — I mean planning — now.

1. Head colds caused by inoperable hairdryers. Count on many of your agents to contract colds when electrical brownouts and blackouts force them to leave the house with wet hair. Many agents will call in sick, leaving you understaffed during a critical peak period. Those who do show up for work will likely be so stuffed up that they'll sound like they've been crying, causing already anxious customers to lose confidence in your company. More sensitive customers will ask sniffling agents, "What's wrong? Do you want to talk about it?" at which time many agents will vent about the crappy presents they received during the holidays, causing talk time to triple.

Head colds will also affect agents' hearing, causing them to respond to questions that callers didn't even ask. For example, a customer calling a gourmet food supply center may inquire, "Do you carry tea?" but the agent might hear, "Will you marry me?" This could lead to a humiliating communication breakdown, or worse—the agent could ask you for two weeks off for the honeymoon.

Two possible solutions to the wet-hair/head cold quandary: 1) Designate January 2000 as "Annual No-Shower Month" in the call center, or 2) Give a substantial bonus to any agents who shave their heads in December.

2. Exhausted agents who party too hard. Y2K is not just about technology and electrical power problems. With all the stress and uncertainty surrounding the Y2K computer glitch, everybody—including your call center agents—is going to be partying like mad on New Year's Eve 1999. Expect most of your staff to be exhausted and/or hungover well into February, which will surely lead to decreased performance and errors in judgment on the phones. It won't be uncommon for agents to enter incorrect information on data screens, forget to confirm names/addresses, and candidly tell customers to call back in March when the nausea, headaches and blurred vision subside.

Such problems will be almost unavoidable because keeping agents from partying like it's 1999 is not really feasible. You may want to consider having a serious discussion with your staff about the dangers of alcohol and the importance of good customer service. Or consider inviting everybody to a "huge New Year's Eve bash" at the call center and, when they show up, lock them in the basement with enough food and water to last them until their next shift.

3. Customers who read the tabloids. Some of the potential call center problems regarding the Y2K issue will begin before the Year 2000 arrives, and the tabloid newspapers will likely be to blame for at least one of them. As your customers begin reading articles about how the Y2K Bug was planted by militant socialist aliens from Mars to destroy our predominantly capitalistic planet, expect to receive more than a few calls, particularly if you work in a financial services call center in California. Gullible customers will take up valuable agent time asking if their money is safe, if the company will cover any losses, and if the aliens can see through clothes. Not only will such repetitive calls make operational costs skyrocket, they will tempt you to tell your coworkers about your UFO encounter in 1993, subjecting you to companywide ridicule and loss of profit-sharing perks.

There is no solution to this potential problem, except to take a side-job as a freelance editor for a major tabloid and replace all Y2K articles with stories about singing llamas.

A Positive Note

I would like to leave you with some good news about Y2K: Call centers with high turnover — those that struggle with the "revolving door" effect of agent attrition — will likely retain more agents in 2000 when the revolving door jams due to a glitch in its programming.

If Dr. Seuss Had Worn a Headset

As much admiration as I have for Dr. Seuss, I can't help but feel that his creative gift was somewhat wasted. He gave far too much coverage to giant talking cats and discolored eggs, and not enough to those aspects of our society that could have truly benefited from his pen.

Call centers are among the things that could have used a P.R. boost from Seuss. (Yeah, I know that he retired before 800 numbers were even invented, but work with me on this one, will ya?) Just think how popular our industry would be had the good doctor taken the time to scribble down a few stories like this one:

"I Will Not Take Incoming Calls"

I will not take incoming calls
I'd rather mop floors at the mall!

How do you know unless you try?
I'm telling you, I'd rather die
I will not take them in the day
There's no way you can make me play
I will not take those calls at night
You must not think I'm very bright

Of course I do, you'd have to be
To take calls from our ACD
Would you take them for good pay?
I'm really understaffed today

I would not take them for good pay
Your staffing problem's here to stay
I would not take calls for an hour
Not for you or Eddie Bauer

Have you ever been a rep?
For your career it's a good step
Won't you answer just one call?
I'm telling you, you'll have a ball

I will not take even just one
To me it doesn't sound like fun
Headsets always hurt my ears
I'm going home to drink some beers

That's just fine, you little devil
You'd probably hurt our service level
I can see that you are weak
And couldn't handle our call peak

Who you calling weak, you putz?
I'll show you who's got the guts
Log me on, I'll take a few
And I'll delight your callers too!
But just so that we're very clear
After these calls I'm outta here

This ain't half bad, in fact it's fine
Helping callers on the line
I can feel the service power
How much do you pay an hour?

Hold on there, friend, not so fast
How do I know that you will last?
High turnover is a pest
I need to hire the very best

I am your man, now that's for sure
Forget those things I said before
I'll meet your goals and stop complaining
I'll always seek ongoing training

Don't make me mop floors at the mall
I want to take incoming calls
I will take them in the day
And keep caller complaints at bay
I will work the night shift, too
Just let me at that blasted queue!

A Brief Criticism of Current Call Center Convention

I'm not one to complain, except when I'm awake, but there are several irksome trends emerging in the call center industry that I'd like to discuss. Now you may be saying to yourself, "Oh great, another liberal youngster who feels he has to question call center authority and challenge the status quo at every turn." That's just not true. Just because I'm an active member of "Reps for Real-Time Revolution (RRTR)" and "Journalists Against Boring Benchmarking (JABB)" doesn't mean that I'm an obsessive rabble-rouser. In fact, I agree with many of the norms in the call center industry, namely quality monitoring, tracking adherence to schedule, and the distribution of free drink tickets at conference cocktail receptions.

However, I feel my strong opinions regarding the issues below must be heard, not just because I feel they are detracting from our industry's success, but because I crave attention.

1. Excessive reverence for the term "call center." I think it is great that call centers have gained so much recognition of late, but many people in the industry are letting their pride mar their grammatical judgment. Every time I peruse an industry-related report, article or white paper, I get queasy over the apparent obsession with capitalizing the term "call center" in sentences where it isn't being used as a proper noun. Examples include: "The Call Center is a very unique place," or "If it weren't for CallCenters (space-removal intentional), the world would end," and then there is the dreaded, "Management now realizes that the CALLCENTER is a strategic weapon."

Yes, call centers have come a long way, but let's keep in mind that they have yet to achieve the status of, say, God, the Internet or Cher, which have earned the right to be capitalized in any context. A little self-restraint, please. Otherwise, every industry is going to start writing this way, and articles on plumbing will contain sentences like, "Today, TOILETS are flushing more efficiently than ever."

2. Lack of consistency in what we call frontline staff. I've written about this before, but the situation has gotten even worse. While there has never been an industrywide term for "the people on the phones," at least the various titles used to be innocent, like "rep" and "CSR." Today we have to contend with insipid monikers like "phone player," "headset hero" and "service level soldier."

I implore every call center manager in the industry to please start using the simple title "agent" to describe the members of their frontline staff. If you support me on this, please call 1-800-GO AGENT. Our Customer Tele-Technicians are standing by to take your call.

3. Deceiving titles for call center conference sessions. While attending an industry event a few months ago, I sat in on a session whose title had caught my attention in the conference brochure. It was called, "10 Surefire Ways to Tackle Turnover and Pump-Up Productivity." Pretty exciting, but when the speaker opened with a slide show of his company parking lot and some irrelevant quotes from Kathy Lee Gifford, I knew he wasn't going to deliver.

Using deceptive session titles to get people in the door at conferences is unfortunately becoming the norm in the industry. Therefore, I suggest implementing a law that requires all conference sessions to have short, unappealing titles like, "Monitoring: An Important Thing," and "Training: Why Not?" This will help to lower attendees' expectations and increase the chances that the speaker's family will see him or her alive again.

4. Obsession with "best practices." How do you get 100 call center professionals to jump off a cliff? Tell them it's a "best practice." Never before has such a meaningless concept been taken so seriously. I must get 20 calls a week from call center professionals who want to know industrywide best-practice objectives for things like service level, abandonment rate and ideal heart-rate during peak seasons. Rather than explain to these managers that industrywide best practices don't exist, I make up answers to scare them out of their fixation: "All the world-class (another meaningless term) call centers I know answer 108 percent of their calls within 11 seconds and have zero abandonment. If any abandonment ever does occur, best-practice call centers require the existing manager to do 200 one-armed pushups on a greased floor."

My advice is for you call center professionals to ignore so-called industrywide best practices and to focus your attention inward to determine what is best for your specific call center based on what your specific customers want and need. You should also avoid cliffs.

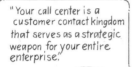

What Conference Speakers Say

What Conference Attendees Hear

ha ha ha ha ha ha ha ha ha ha ha ha ha ha ha

Call Center Q & A

A recent subscriber phone survey conducted by *Call Center Management Review* revealed some interesting findings. For instance, we found that most of you often dream about the attractive models used in headset ads, and that only a few of you permit agents to practice the clarinet at their seats when they are not on a call.

The survey also indicated that you want to see even more "how-to" articles to help you tackle the tough call center challenges you face each day. You want more expert advice on forecasting and scheduling, hiring, monitoring and removing those unsightly hairs from your IVR.

In response to your requests for more how-to information, I've decided to occasionally dedicate my column to a "Question & Answer" forum on important call center topics. Here's how it works: You send me your questions; I conduct rigorous research to uncover accurate and insightful responses; you read the responses and stand in awe of my knowledge.

Question:

I have a big problem with agent turnover at my call center. I've tried numerous incentive ideas, but nothing seems to work. What do you suggest?

Answer:

In my experience, the best way to keep agents happy and working for you is to let them do whatever they please. Too many call center managers expect agents to answer all the calls, meet certain goals, dress a certain way, show up for work, bathe. With all those rules, can you blame agents for leaving?

It's a tough job, so why not give agents the freedom to ignore adherence objectives, make unlimited personal calls and swear at annoying customers? Such an approach may not help your service levels or caller satisfaction results, but it will show agents that you truly respect them as individuals. And that respect will keep them working at your call center for a long time, or at least until an angry mob of neglected customers torches the place.

Question:

I manage a call center for a small company with a limited budget for technology. How can I ensure world-class service with second-rate equipment?

Answer:

You don't need advanced technology to achieve impressive results in your call center; you need creativity and ingenuity, or agents who don't require sleep. Don't listen to what all the vendors say you need. The benefits of most of the latest technology can be realized via much less expensive means.

Take CTI for example. You don't need a bunch of fancy equipment to tell agents who is calling and why before the call is connected; instead hire agents with ESP. If you are willing to look past the strange clothes and makeup worn by most people with psychic powers, you'll be able to freely tap into this unique and valuable labor pool.

And who needs an expensive IVR system? Just bring your kids and those of your coworkers into the call center to greet callers, tell them their routing options, and entertain them until an agent is available. Most customers prefer live-answer and everybody loves children. The only drawback is that you'll have to take your kids out of school, which is illegal, but at least you won't have to worry about them hanging out with the wrong crowd—unless they befriend members of accounting.

Question:

I hear a lot of call center managers talking about "best practices." What exactly does "best practice" mean?

Answer:

The easiest way for me to define this popular term is to use it in a sentence: "If you don't already know how to ignore colleagues who incessantly use empty buzzwords, you 'best practice.'"

Publisher's Note: The advice provided in this column represents the thoughts and opinions of Greg Levin and not necessarily those of a stable, fully functioning member of society.

More Call Center Q & A (as Promised)

Since the publication of the original "Call Center Q & A" column, I received nominations for various prestigious industry awards, including "Best Q & A Call Center Journalist under 5′ 10″" and the "Nobel Prize for Call Center Literature." You may not have heard of them, but that doesn't make them any less real to me.

Well, I've never been one to let success go to my head—as if I'd have time, what with all the photo shoots and lunches with really important people. Nope, I realize the most important thing is to keep my promise and continue to provide solid advice to curious call center professionals.

So, keep your questions coming and I'll keep answering them. The only difference is that I will now charge a modest fee of $2,000 for each response.

Question:

Senior management recently asked me to develop a formal customer satisfaction measurement program for our call center. What is the best way to go about this?

Answer:

First, let's get one thing clear—customer satisfaction numbers aren't always an accurate representation of your call center's success. For instance, I've known call centers with a customer satisfaction rating of 98 percent that have exorbitant turnover, generate little to no revenue, and have horrible Chicken Piccata in the cafeteria. On the contrary, I've also known call centers with only a 75 percent satisfaction rating that have... actually, those centers pretty much stank, too.

But back to your question: The best way to go about measuring customer satisfaction in a way that will impress the suits upstairs is to contract with a fictional customer research firm, then make up the results yourself. The benefits of contracting with a make-believe research firm are lower costs, less travel time and the ease of ending the partnership if you're not satisfied with their work.

Note: When making up the customer satisfaction rating to show senior management, I recommend staying within the 90 to 93 percent range. Anything higher may earn your center industry awards and accolades — and that just wouldn't be ethical.

Question:

Many of our agents complain that our monitoring criteria are too subjective and that evaluation scores don't always reflect their true performance. How can I overcome agents' monitoring apprehension?

Answer:

You can start by telling them that they should be grateful for any monitoring they receive, reminding them that there are poor agents in other parts of the world who often go months or years without being monitored.

That's the problem with the younger generation in the Western world today — they don't appreciate how good they have it. "I want more objective criteria." "I want positive feedback." "I want a headset that doesn't make my ears bleed." It's always "me, me, me" with them. I suggest you sit down with agents and tell them about how — back when you were an agent — monitoring was conducted by angry warlords in cold cages with dirt floors, and that feedback came in the form of sharp pokes in the side with a spear. And tell them that you were happy to get those sharp pokes. If that doesn't change your agents' perspective, you may want to reevaluate your hiring practices.

Question:

Lately I've been encountering a serious staffing drought in our call center. What can I do to attract qualified agents?

Answer:

You may want to consider making the actual agent job more appealing. Remember, agents are just like anybody else, except that they are more inclined to shudder and break into frantic tears whenever their home phone rings.

Since agents are similar to your average person, if you want to attract them to and keep them in the call center, you need to offer them the things that the average person desires. With that in mind, start by equipping all workstations with Lazyboy recliners and color TVs; adding a mall food court to the call center; offering scream therapy during stressful periods; and letting them balance house plants on their head while humming (or is it just me who likes to do that?).

Ambiguous Feedback

ha ha ha ha ha ha ha ha ha ha ha ha ha ha ha

Diary of an Agent Meltdown

Nobody could have predicted the emotional meltdown of Twyla Benson, veteran phone agent for Louisiana Light and Electric (LLE). She had endured numerous call deluges during power outages in the past without so much as a whimper or a whine. Her fellow agents revered her dedication, confidence and unique ability to gracefully remove her headset without using her hands.

Twyla always seemed invincible, until the afternoon of July 16, 1998. In the midst of taking calls during a weeklong tropical storm that left 50 percent of LLE's customers without power, Twyla suddenly snapped. She stood up from her workstation, head-butted her computer screen, threw her chair at the call center readerboard and screamed, "Use candles, you redneck!!!" to the customer on the phone. Twyla then bit off her headset mouthpiece, dropped to the floor and started barking. Her colleagues were shocked—never before had they heard Twyla forget to confirm a caller's last name.

Twyla's supervisor recently discovered a journal that Twyla had been keeping during the week of the fateful storm. The journal entries provide a fascinating account of the sad unraveling of the center's top agent, who has since moved on to a circus career under the stage name of "Dog Girl."

Monday, July 13 — 4:30 p.m.

High winds and heavy rain have left many of our poor customers in the dark. I'm handling about 50 calls an hour—I just wish I could do more. All those nice people trying to get through to us for information and consolation. I love them all like family. My manager just offered me some pizza, but I told him I couldn't possibly take time to eat while our customers are suffering so. I think I'll volunteer to work through the night.

Tuesday, July 14 — 11:15 a.m.

Call after call after call. Things sure are crazy around here, but that's why I became a phone rep. I live for helping customers in need. Granted, it would be easier if they didn't yell at me whenever I answer the phone. Don't they know that I didn't ask for this tropical storm? Don't they know that I'm on their side? Probably not—most of them don't even know their own zip code. Oops, that was mean and uncalled for. Must stay focused. I wonder if there is any leftover pizza from yesterday.

Tuesday, July 14 — 5:40 p.m.

I've handled 120 calls in the past hour and a half. Can't get my left eyelid to stop twitching. I'm starting to regret not going to work on my father's farm. No phones. No confining workstations. Just fresh air and plenty of nice goats.

Wednesday, July 15 — 9:50 a.m.

My supervisor just hung a banner in the center of the phone floor that says "Don't Give Up." How encouraging. I should hang him from the center of the phone floor by his ugly tie. Oh, but then who would monitor my every action? As I write this, an annoying caller is babbling into my ear—something about a down power line in her backyard. I just told her that a technician would be there as soon as possible, and I recommended that she go out and mow her lawn in the meantime. She hung up. But what's this? Surprise! Another call is coming in. Probably just Satan.

Thursday, July 16—I don't know what time it is

The rain will never stop. The calls will never stop. My eyelid twitch will never stop, and I can't even collect disability pay for it. All the customers are out to get me, I know it. They're out there plotting ways to have their calls routed directly to me. They want to see me crack, but I refuse to let them destroy me. They have no idea of the powers I possess. They may be able to take away my lunch break, but they will never defeat me! For I am "Twyla—Queen of the Queue!" I'm invincible! Aha ha ha ha ha ha ha!

That was Twyla's last journal entry before her complete breakdown. Three supervisors tried to restrain her when she became violent, but her strength overwhelmed them. The struggle didn't stop until the call center manager shot Twyla with one of the tranquilizer darts that the center often uses on agents who are unhappy with their holiday bonus.

Call Center—The Movie

ha ha ha ha ha ha ha ha ha ha ha ha ha ha

Loners on Phones

When hiring agents, call center professionals naturally seek qualified candidates who will be likely to stick around for a while to handle calls. But most managers go about this all wrong. They make the mistake of hiring emotionally well-adjusted, energetic people who possess "winning" personalities and much ambition. Such agents are often promoted out of the call center or become TV weather reporters before managers even learn their names.

If you really want to tackle turnover and reduce churn, you have to seek loners — social malcontents who just want to be left alone to handle calls in their comfortable little workstations for years on end. For example, Meg Ryan would not have lasted long as a phone rep; Bob Dylan, with a little speech therapy, would have.

Here is a list of the specific benefits of hiring loners to work in your call center:

1. Reduced costs. The dollar savings that result from investing in loner agents can have a significant impact on your company's bottom line. For example, loners generally lack career ambitions and are thus likely to stay put in the call center for years on end. Because you will rarely have to replace them, the costs of recruiting and training will drop dramatically. In addition, loners will often work for less money because they don't have a strong interest in material items, such as nice cars, designer clothes or toothpaste.

2. More flexible scheduling. From a call center perspective, one of the greatest qualities of loners is their lack of friends. Agents with such nonexistent social lives cause managers in charge of scheduling to jump for joy. Loners never offer excuses such as "I can't work that night, I have a date" or "That weekend's not good for me — my best friend is getting married." Working evenings, weekends and holidays is not only acceptable to loners, it's preferred. For example, they'd rather occupy their time on Christmas Day handling call after call than sitting at home alone watching "clay-mation" specials on TV while experiencing painful memories of when their mothers forced them to sit on Santa's lap at the mall when they were seven.

3. Less resistance to monitoring feedback. Tired of dealing with defensive agents who argue and whine whenever you try to give them some constructive feedback following a monitoring session? Loner agents know that complaining and debating with you and your supervisors will only draw more unwanted attention to them. So not only will loners listen quietly to suggestions for improvement, they will likely act on it quickly to help eliminate the need for any lengthy conversation with you in the future. (Tip: Use remote monitoring or taped calls whenever evaluating loners — side-by-side monitoring causes them to experience heart palpitations and/or nosebleeds, which often diminish the quality of the call.)

4. Improved adherence to schedule. If you staff your call center with loner agents, I guarantee you will see a dramatic improvement in adherence to schedule statistics. These employees don't want to spend any more time than necessary in the break room interacting with live people, so they'll always return quickly from breaks — many won't even take them. About the only time they will ever be out of adherence is if they happen to be reading a book by Jean-Paul Sartre during lunch and lose track of time while contemplating the absurd meaninglessness of human existence and ACD reports.

5. Less office gossip. Fed up with agents wasting time spreading rumors about who's dating whom in the office, whose marriages are breaking up, and which supervisor is actually a weekend professional wrestler named "The Masked Monitorer"? You won't have to worry about such insipid chit-chat if you hire people who would rather extract their toenails with a dull Swiss Army knife than engage in informal dialogue with coworkers. Not only will your call center be more productive, you won't need to worry about your secret love of Chia Pets being revealed by rumoring employees.

Call Routing on the Edge

Call centers are starting to break free from the confines and rigidity of simple call routing. Until recently, callers — regardless of who they are or what they want — have been blindly sent to the next available agent at most centers. Today, however, many progressive call centers are exploring call-routing methods that are so unconventional, they have been banned in China and certain Midwestern U.S. cities. These unique methods are worthy of attention, for they may lead to revolutionary change in our industry or, at the very least, to an investigative piece on *60 Minutes*.

Here are what some call centers are doing in the area of innovative call routing to enhance service, reduce operating costs and make you feel behind the times.

HMOKAY HEALTH INSURANCE
Hartford, Connecticut

HMOkay uses priority queuing like no other call center on earth or in Southern California. The center's New Policy division gives priority to seemingly healthy callers because they cost less to cover and don't whine to agents. Every call is front-ended by an IVR system that helps to determine if new callers have any serious health risks. A voice prompt asks callers such questions as "Do you smoke?" "Do you drink?" and "Do your kids attend public school?" Callers who answer "no" to all risk assessment questions are quickly routed to a live agent anxious to sell a policy. Callers who answer "yes" to one or two questions are knocked back a few places in the queue. Those who answer "yes" to three or four questions are placed at the end of the queue. And those who answer "yes" to five or more questions are immediately routed to a company competitor or to a hospital.

The IVR system also has been programmed to listen for any sneezing, coughing or wheezing sounds to help determine a caller's health. If any such sounds are detected, a voice prompt says "Gesundheit!" or "Cover your mouth when you do that!" before the caller is bumped back in the queue.

MEGAMERCHANDISE
Chicago, Illinios

MegaMerchandise, which offers everything from saucepans to sporting goods, knows that customers appreciate the personal touch. The call center — staffed with an eclectic group of employees — uses a truly unique routing process that matches each caller with an agent who has similar interests, personality traits or SAT scores.

All calls are initially answered by one of 20 live agents — called "matchmakers" — whose job is to quickly assess which agent the caller is most likely to bond with. For instance, if a man from Brooklyn calls interested in purchasing a baseball bat or a thick metal chain, the matchmaker will route that call to an agent like Joey "No-Neck" Marini. Joey can then have a friendly informal chat with the caller about scars and broken kneecaps before closing the certain sale. Or if a customer calls without a clue as to what they want, the matchmaker would likely route the call to an agent who doesn't have a clue as to what they are doing.

BIG SPUR BANK AND MISTRUST
Sweetwater, Texas

Handling irate customers is never fun, but routing them to convicted killers can be. Big Spur Bank has been doing it for about a year with impressive results. The bank call center uses cutting-edge technology to identify angry callers, who are then automatically routed to death-row inmates trained to help callers realize the relative pettiness of their complaints.

Here's how it works. The center's automated attendant is able to measure the heart rate of each caller. Whenever the rate exceeds 200 beats per minute, the automated attendant knows that the caller is either furious or has just run a 10K. To determine which is the case, the caller is asked to press 1 if they are "fighting mad" or to press 2 if they need Gatorade. Callers who press 1 are seamlessly routed to the first available murderer in one of the many fine high-security prisons in Texas. Inmates use phrases like "How dare you complain to me about a finance charge — I have to eat gruel every night" or "You think having your loan request denied is bad, try sleeping on a metal cot knowing that you have only two months to live!" In most cases, callers calm down and apologize for their selfishness. The inmate can then take advantage of the caller's guilt by cross-selling additional bank products.

Prehistoric VRUs

ha ha ha ha ha ha ha ha ha ha ha ha ha ha ha

An Uncensored Guide to Vendor Selection

Selecting technology vendors with whom to do business can be one of the most unnerving experiences of a call center professional's career—second perhaps only to having to hide all the agent whips whenever OSHA comes around for an inspection. Not to generalize, but every call center technology vendor on the planet is deceptive and dangerous. You must be armed with knowledge and cunning — and sometimes actual weapons — before meeting with a vendor to discuss what they and their product can do for your call center.

Here are some suggestions on how best to emerge from the vendor selection process relatively unscathed. Keep in mind, I'm off my medication.

1. Approach all vendors as if they were used car salesmen. I'm not implying that every vendor is pushy and lies a lot, just the ones that speak. To help you measure the amount of truth in each vendor statement, take the number of positive adjectives used to describe the product, and multiply that figure by the number of Ethiopian Sumo wrestling champions in the world.

It's important to learn as much as possible about the product before talking to a vendor salesperson and to ask tough questions that let him or her know that you are not going to be jerked around. Counter all their attempts to soften you up for the sale. For example, if they say things like, "Wow, you're pretty sharp, I can see you've done your homework," tell them that actually you never finished grade school and that you aren't sure if you want to do business with such a poor judge of character.

2. Test the vendor's integrity. Tell the vendor you'll purchase their product if they'll throw their mother in for free. Those who comply would obviously do or say anything to get you to buy and thus should be crossed off your list, unless, of course, their mother happens to be filthy rich.

3. Laugh good and hard at the price. This usually catches vendors off guard, though you'd think they'd be used to the laughter by now.

Salespeople have fragile egos and hate being scoffed at, and so will usually come down in price just to shut you up. If they say that they can't lower the price because they are barely making a profit as it is, ask how they were then able to afford an exhibit booth with its own zip code and mayor at the last trade show.

4. Survey current users of the product in person. Once you've narrowed your vendor choices to two or three, ask each for a list of current call center clients for you to contact. If at all possible, visit each user's call center rather than conducting a simple phone survey. This way you can see for yourself that the contact is a real call center manager and not the vendor salesperson's slick Cousin Joey who's well versed on the product's alleged benefits. During your site visit, ask users if they highly recommend, recommend or do not recommend the product and, most importantly, if you can take a small blood sample to ensure that they aren't related to any employees of the vendor in question.

5. Start dating one of the vendor salespeople. After you've decided which vendor you are going to go with, and before you actually purchase the product, begin a romantic relationship with a salesperson from that company. This may seem desperate and extreme, but your call center's bottom line is at stake. After a few candlelit dinners and quiet talks about secret pleasures and the sex appeal of CTI, your new mate will likely feel very shallow making you pay for the product he or she is pedaling. While your current spouse or significant other may leave you forever and curse you until the day you die, you'll be able to rest assured that the money you saved your call center enabled the CEO of your company to buy the condo in Aspen he's always wanted.

Publisher's Note: The views expressed above by Greg do not necessarily reflect the views of anybody who was ever given a toy as a child. Vendors reading this article should not be too concerned that the advice provided by Greg will be taken seriously by any RESPECTABLE call center professionals. What vendors should be concerned about is the fact that call center professionals who read Greg's column each month generally aren't interested in respectability.

Call Center Daycare: A New Approach to Recruiting and Training

Your struggle with finding and keeping qualified agents may finally be over.

What's the answer to your frontline woes? How about a call center daycare program that combines nurturing attention with early agent training for your employees' children? It's perfect! It gives workers an affordable childcare option while paving the way for a powerful private labor pool at your call center for years to come. Think about it: Would your employees rather have their children sitting at home with a nanny watching dangerously manipulative television shows like *Sesame Street* and *Barney,* or near their parents in the call center receiving unconditional affection while learning valuable cross-selling skills?

Before you cancel your subscription and report me to the proper authorities, allow me to further explain the various components of my proposed call center daycare program.

1. Play time. Children are supplied with numerous games and toys to keep them from sitting idle. Each child is required to be engaged in some type of fun activity 25 out of the 30 minutes allotted for the play-time shift. Those who do not adhere to this schedule lose cookie privileges for the day. Games such as "Operation" and others that feature minor electric shocks/loud buzzers are provided to help the future agents learn to deal with high stress levels early on in their lives. Children are encouraged to play in groups to help build teamwork skills and to reduce wait times for toys. Daycare supervisors closely observe each child's behavior to ensure quality playtime, providing immediate feedback to hair-pullers and glue-eaters. Occasionally, each child is placed alone in a room and told to play as usual; those who adapt well to such alienation are looked at as future telecommuter candidates.

2. Finger painting. During this unique session, each child is paired with a partner and supplied with finger paints, paper and role-play scripts (this exercise only works with children old enough to read). While one child prepares to paint, the other reads questions/statements from the script, like "Hi, I'm (name), may I have your name, please?" (teaches customer-greeting skills); "What color paint would you like today?" (probing skills); "Could I interest you in some green — it's one of my favorite colors?" (soft-selling skills); and the all-important "Aaaw, I see you got paint all over your new *Teletubbies* t-shirt — I understand how upset you must be" (empathy skills). Children who struggle with any of these skill areas receive one-on-one instruction from either a daycare supervisor or an experienced peer.

3. Story time. Here, supervisors read famous children's books that have been modified for the call center daycare program. Among the most popular and effective stories are *The Little Agent Who Could, The Cat in the Headset, Curious George Gets Carpal Tunnel, Clifford Clears the Queue* and, for the more advanced children, *Charlotte's Web-Enabled Call Center*.

4. Mommy monitoring. This session enables supervisors to keep children from missing their mothers while teaching them what comprises a quality customer transaction. Each child sits on the lap of a supervisor and listens in while the supervisor monitors the child's mother on a call. Seatbelts are used to strap the child in with the supervisor for two reasons: 1) It keeps children who become over-excited by their mother's voice from running out onto the phone floor in search of her; and 2) It helps children become accustomed to the fact that, in the call center, there is nowhere to run. Children whose mothers receive poor monitoring scores are instructed to "give mommy constructive feedback" during the car ride home. This helps each child develop important supervisory skills and saves the real supervisors the pain of having to tell the mother that her performance blew.

Recommendations

Those of you who decide to adopt my daycare program should consider a few suggestions to enhance its effectiveness. For instance, ask parents to occasionally bring their kids in on Saturdays to help the children get used to weekend shifts while they are young. Also, ask parents to pick their child up late once in awhile, as it's never to soon to prepare future agents for overtime.

Bob Tries a More Flexible Staffing Strategy

ha ha ha ha ha ha ha ha ha ha ha ha ha ha ha

Nostradamus' Own Form of Forecasting

Most of you have heard of Nostradamus — the 16th century prophet who predicted such ominous events as World War I, Hitler's reign and the creation of the "new" Coca-Cola. But did you know that the great seer also predicted the development of the call center industry? It's true. In 1554, Nostradamus wrote: "The 1970s and 1980s will be marked by evil music, evil hair and the demand for efficient service from underpaid people who work in 'cubes' and speak into tools called 'fones.'"

Nostradamus made numerous other call center-related predictions, many of which have come true and many of which still may.

Here are just a few of the great prophet's industry-related predictions. All were made between the years 1554 and 1562 (1562 was the year Nostradamus' mother kicked him out of the house and insisted he get a real job):

1980: A wise American man of Scottish descent will invent the term "caul centre" to refer to the place where the underpaid cube people using fones help public demanders. Years will pass before the term becomes accepted by the ruling classes, who will then sell flimsy reports exploiting the concept.

1982: Those who oversee the caul centre will discover that hitting the cube people over the head and screaming "Faster! Faster!" does not increase production. As a result, the overseers will add more cube people to the caul centre and teach them all to focus less on mere production and more on serving the needs of the public demanders, however irritating such individuals may be. Sweets and other culinary items will start being used extensively by the overseers to lure the cube people into submission, reducing attrition, though fostering weight gain.

1986: Despite overseers' efforts, hordes of cube people will leave the caul centre in search of a less stressful environment and one that earns them more respect from the ruling classes. Many overseers will respond by throwing up their hands in defeat and obsessing over the futility of human existence. More committed overseers will entice cube people to enter and remain in the caul centre by improving conditions and creating opportunities for advancement into the echelons of the ruling classes. Among the caul centre improvements will be better instruction, more advanced tools and the advent of such rewards as "Cube Person of the Month."

1992: The entire caul centre industry will nearly come crashing down under the weight of all its acronyms. Letter combinations such as "ACD," "CTI," "TSR" and "ASA" will help to shorten memos, but cause severe neurological dysfunction among readers. Debate over which acronym — "IVR," "VRU" or "ARS" — best describes a certain type of tool will lead to physical struggles and bloodshed. Almost all possible letter combinations will be exhausted, but rather than cease the creation of acronyms, caul centre people will ask the government to add new letters to the alphabet.

1996: Most of the world will become enthralled with an advanced research tool invented by scientists called the Hinternett. Caul centre product merchants will develop propaganda telling caul centre overseers that they will become extinct unless they connect their centre to this powerful Hinternett. Most overseers will not buy into the elaborate world of false Hinternett realities created by the merchants. However, the few who do will pay an astronomical amount of money for products, providing merchants with enough capital to create more Hinternett propaganda and to afford suits made of the finest Mediterranean fabric.

2001: Extreme obsession with "best practices" proposed by invalid research reports will lead to the demise of the entire industry, forcing most people into careers in the food and beverage industry or real estate. These reports will entice caul centres hungry for simplistic standards to blindly adopt methods and procedures that have little or nothing to do with their specific caul centre. After the industry's extinction, most caul centre structures will be taken over by a powerful mouse-faced man named Gates, who will convert them into prisons to house all his potential competitors.

To order a complete listing of Nostradamus' call center predictions, please call Prophets for Profits at 800-555-DOOM. The first 100 call center professionals who call will also receive a free booklet listing the names of their agents who are going to quit within the next year.

Benchmark Efforts

ha ha ha ha ha ha ha ha ha ha ha ha ha ha ha

Spicing Up the Agent Image

Many call center professionals have told me that they are struggling more than ever to attract qualified agent applicants. My typical piece of advice, "Wear something sexy" — which, by the way, used to get big laughs — now causes managers to merely growl and tell me to grow up. They're fed up with having to recruit from a shallow labor pool, and even my sophisticated wit isn't enough to get them to crack a smile anymore.

The big problem is the negative image that most young people have of call center work: Sitting in small, gray cubicles while wearing an uncomfortable headset and answering call after call after call for hours on end, with little room for advancement. But that's such a distorted view. For instance, some cubicles today are a nice shade of blue.

Okay, let's face it, as rewarding as call center work may be, on the surface it's not that alluring to college graduates or others with strong communication skills and serious debt. Here are some suggestions to help spice up the industry image and enhance the chances of you having to tell alumni from schools like Stanford and Brown that you'll keep their resume on file in case an agent position opens up.

1. Provide "alternative" headsets. Many young people feel that wearing a headset is a sign of failure, an indication that they are just a lowly "operator" lacking any real skills. They fail to realize that 1) being a call center agent requires numerous important skills; 2) even CEOs wear headsets during long calls to avoid stiff necks; and 3) four out of five medical doctors surveyed say that wearing a headset significantly decreases the chances of having a bee fly into your ear while on the job.

But rather than try to overcome the general public's negative view of headsets, why not replace the devices with something that doesn't really look like a headset? For example, you could decorate each headset with fake diamonds, rubies and emeralds. Then, whenever you meet reluctant applicants who feel they are "above" call center work, you can tell them they'll get to wear a bejeweled crown to fit their royal self-image.

2. Break up the monotony. Most people are turned off by call center work because the thought of handling calls from the average Joe all day long makes them yawn. They want something more exciting and unpredictable. I say give them what they want. Do creative things like occasionally hiring an actor to play a disgruntled customer who runs into the call center screaming obscenities and threatening the life of any agent who moves from his seat. This will not only get staff's adrenaline pumping and make them tell their friends (potential applicants) how invigorating their job is, it will reduce the amount of "wandering" agents engage in, thus improving adherence-to-schedule statistics.

Other easy ways to inject excitement into the agents' call center routine include 1) sponsoring unannounced "nude supervisor" days; 2) releasing a rabid wolverine on the phone floor; and 3) moving the call center to Rio during the Carnival.

3. Create a sitcom about agents in a call center. One of the best ways to attract young people to call center work is to make it the subject of a hit comedy TV sitcom, preferably starring Michael Richards from *Seinfeld* as the zany lead agent. I urge call center professionals throughout the industry to get together and create such a show, and call it something like *Mad About Queue* or *Ain't Life a Kick in the Headset*. All that's needed is about 10 good-looking mediocre actors wearing cool clothes, a New York City or Los Angeles setting, some call center props and, of course, a rabid wolverine or two.

Each episode could highlight typical call center occurrences, with a little embellishment to enhance ratings. For instance, the pilot episode could be about how the agents — struggling to handle the call volume — kidnap the CEO's wife and golf clubs until he agrees to staffing increases.

I recommend contacting the head of the Fox Television Network to get this baby on TV. There should be no problem winning his approval, provided that you follow the Fox formula and promise that all characters will sleep with one another before the end of the first season.

Note: If all else fails in your attempts to attract hordes of agent applicants, consider paying off the Surgeon General to declare that NOT handling dozens of calls a day from customers can cause baldness and bad breath.

Call Center Obituaries

Every year just after Halloween, I become temporarily fixated on two things: leftover Snickers bars and death. And since it's difficult to incorporate Snickers bars into a call center-related article (unless I were to discuss how many calls the Mars Candy Co. receives from customers wanting to know what, exactly, is "nougat"), I've decided to write about death this month.

So how does one tactfully tie death into a call center column, you may ask? By listing the obituaries of those respected members of our industry who have passed away recently. Oh, wipe that scornful look off your face—you know you are just as intrigued by obituaries as I am, especially those of you who are apartment-hunting in the city.

Here are just a few obits to honor those call center professionals who recently have been routed to a better place with shorter hold times:

ROBERT SIMMONS, 54

Call Center Director

TO AIR IS HUMAN TRAVEL CO.

Robert Simmons, the customer service pioneer who coined the phrase, "Yikes! There are 100 calls in queue—we're doomed!" passed away last weekend while looking for parking outside his Boston call center. He was described by friends and coworkers as a courageous and kind man who always lent a sympathetic ear, except during the peak season, when he usually just ran around and yelled a lot.

Prior to becoming director of To Air Is Human's call center, Robert spent 12 years managing a service bureau, where he received numerous accolades for his ability to fit three agents into each workstation.

He is survived by his wife, two children, three managers, eight supervisors and 124 agents.

ETHEL JOHNSON, 68

Customer Service Manager

MIS MANAGED HEALTH CARE

Ethel Johnson, one of the most beloved and shortest professionals in the call center industry, died suddenly of heart failure in her office this week while looking at the call center budget that senior management had just handed down. Throughout her career she was a strong proponent for agents' rights; her most noteworthy victory came when she succeeded in lowering the number of times agents could be spanked by frustrated supervisors from five times a week to three.

Ethel was offered a generous retirement package at age 65, but the committed, forever-young manager chose not to end her career. Some say she refused to leave the call center to continue fighting against poor agent compensation; others say it was because she couldn't find her keys.

Ethel is survived by her three children, four supervisors, 65 agents, and her pet iguana "Rep-Tile."

STEPHEN FISCHBEIN, 51

Call Center Manager

SAPTOV ENERGY

Stephen Fischbein, "the man who made headsets hip" after appearing on the cover of *GQ*'s "Special Call Center Issue" in 1993, died Monday of complications resulting from a long battle with a customer disputing her bill. Stephen was known for being anything but conventional with his management methods. Soon after coming on board he replaced the center's peer monitoring program with a beer monitoring program, where agents were permitted to relax with a few cold ones prior to having their calls evaluated. As a result, agent turnover and morale improved, though their liver functions reportedly worsened.

Stephen's colleagues held a special service at the call center to honor him last night. "Stephen will be dearly missed," said his tearful boss. "He always thought 'out of the box,' except for the time he hid in a shipping crate after the call center's mainframe crashed."

Stephen is survived by his best friend's girlfriend, two supervisors and 32 agents.

ANN MCDUGAL, 92
Senior Agent
BANK OF MERGERS

Ann McDugal, the oldest active call center agent… um, actually, Ann hasn't died yet, but I needed something to fill the last few lines of this column. There, that should do it. We'll get Ann the next time around.

Dracula as a Call Center Agent

Living Up to Your "Next Millennium Manager" Moniker

The fact that you are reading this book most likely means one of two things: 1) Your call center survived the Y2K bug and is still standing; or 2) You are my mother, who reads all of my columns and then calls to apologize profusely for dropping me as a child.

Those of you who fall into category #1, congratulations! But there is no time to rest on your laurels; you are now officially a "Next Millennium" call center professional and have to live up to your esteemed title.

Here is a list of the progressive call center issues that you will need to focus on during the first part of this century if you want to be successful. Those of you who want to be unsuccessful should ignore these issues, stop wearing pants to work and encourage agents to play Yahtzee in the training room during peak calling periods.

1. Staff sharing. With so much call center growth, qualified agents are being snatched up quicker than government scientists can clone them. As a result, managers need to be creative and resourceful to staff their centers effectively.

Sharing agents with compatible call centers in your region is one of the best ways to economically manage peak periods and to enable your agents to sample a more diverse range of cafeteria fare. The problem is that many call center managers think that sharing staff with other companies is too radical, so even if you are interested in exploring the option, it's difficult to find centers with which to partner.

The best way to handle this is to spend time educating colleagues on the huge potential benefits of sharing staff. If they still seem resistant, simply scream "Scaredy cat! Scaredy cat!" in their faces until they cave.

Here is some advice to follow when choosing a call center with which to form a staff-sharing alliance. 1) Ensure that your busy season occurs during months when business at their center is slow, and vice versa. 2) Seek companies that have no competitive link with yours. 3) Seek companies that pay agents similar to what you pay yours. 4) Ensure that their manager has never served time for kidnapping.

2. Video over Internet protocol (IP) technology. Most companies have integrated their call centers with the Internet, whether via e-mail, text-chat, Web callback or voice-over-IP applications. But few organizations have taken their Web centers to the next level, which involves enabling customers not only to write to and speak to live agents online, but to see them and give them the finger when arguing about a billing statement. Video over IP technology not only ensures more personal service and enhances customer satisfaction, it inspires agents to bathe more regularly to look nice on camera. Prior to implementing a video over IP application in your call center, be sure to provide agents with training to help them break common phone habits — e.g., yawning, rolling eyes, and circling "help wanted" ads in the newspaper — that can hinder a customer video transaction.

A few pioneer call centers are taking video over IP applications one step further — adding odor-over-IP technology that enables agents to soften up customers with such personal greetings as, "Hi, my name's John and you smell GREAT!"

3. Real customer relationship management. One of the hottest call center trends today is Customer Relationship Management (also referred to as "Customer Information Management," "Customer Management Solutions," and, to close friends, "Bob"). Everybody knows that, with so much competition and parity among companies these days, dazzling valuable customers with personalized service and establishing strong bonds with them is essential.

To do so, I feel that managers need to expand the boundaries of customer service beyond the confines of the call center. For example, offer bonuses to agents who date or marry callers — or both — to enhance customer relationships. Or hire your agents out as baby-sitters to local customers on weekends (not recommended if you are in a union environment). And to help build rapport with wealthy business clients, require all agents to take golf lessons, drink cognac and own a timeshare in Hilton Head. (To assist agents who can't afford these things, tie in creative call center incentives such as a "putting-based pay" program.)

Start a Revolution

Remember, being a successful next-generation call center professional requires you to take risks. Question normalcy. Challenge authority. Wear white pants after Labor Day.

Don't be afraid to start a call center revolution, but be sure to follow the steps listed in the "dissenters and dissidents" section of your company's employee manual.

A Truly Helpful Call Center Vendor Emerges

Creative Ways to Get Senior Management's Attention

Despite the growth and accomplishments that the call center industry has enjoyed in recent years, most managers say that they still don't have the "ear" of senior management. These call center managers point to staffing shortages, inferior technology and shag carpeting on the phone floor as evidence that their centers aren't receiving the support they need at the executive level.

Getting the attention of senior management can often be accomplished without violent tactics. Here are some innovative ways that you can quickly get your CEO to drop his or her putter and start focusing on the call center's needs.

1. Hold their secretaries for ransom. While rarely listed in any "best practice" reports, kidnapping your CEO's secretary (a.k.a. "office assistant," "executive administrator" or "life support") is the best way to set up your call center success. Without their secretaries, most CEOs are reduced to insecure, panicky creatures who will usually agree to anything to restore order in their office, provided it doesn't involve flying coach class.

Once you have his or her secretary in captivity, send your CEO an anonymous note stating that the secretary will be returned only after the following demands are met: 1) The call center's staffing budget is doubled; 2) agents' dumb terminals are replaced with multimedia PCs; 3) the center gets its own full-time masseuse; and 4) the CEO and marketing director promise to carry the call center manager around on a velvet throne at the next holiday party while singing: "Did you ever know you were my hero."

Note: Consider outsourcing the kidnapping duties to a professional to reduce the risk of getting caught and spending the rest of your life on death row. Such a mishap can be devastating to your call center's quality efforts, as few prisons will allow you to monitor agents remotely.

2. Place subliminal messages in the "stock quote" section of The *Wall Street Journal.* This less-innovative though more-legal approach combines the allure of capitalism with the power of suggestion.

CEOs and other senior officers spend hours on end reading stock quotes in the paper (and high-fiving one another), so why not use this opportunity to "advertise" your call center's needs? Call the classified ad department of The *Wall Street Journal* and arrange to have a few strategic, subliminal phrases printed between the lines on the stock pages. Brief messages such as "20 more agents now," "CTI for Christmas" and "the call center is the messiah" should do the trick.

And don't be afraid to have some fun with this approach; in addition to the phrases listed above, try less-business-related ones such as "challenge Mike Tyson to a fight" or "go swimming only a few minutes after eating."

3. Route overflow calls to their cell phones on the golf course. To truly make senior execs understand what your call center is up against, try to place them directly in your agents' shoes. Consider paying off one of your telecom people to route all calls in queue to senior execs' cell phones while they're out golfing. This will show upper management how drastically understaffed your call center is, and the constant ringing will throw off their back swing, causing them to give up golf altogether and spend more time reading The *Wall Street Journal* (where their minds can be molded by your subliminal tactics).

4. Promise to be their chauffeur if they attend a call center management conference. Okay, okay... so you think kidnapping is immoral, you think subliminal messages don't work (subscribe to *CCMReview*), and you like it when the executives go golfing so that you and your staff can play Twister on the phone floor during low-volume periods. Well, the only other way to make senior managers empathetic to the call center's needs is to have them attend a reputable industry conference where they can pay thousands of dollars to learn all the stuff you've been telling them for free all these years.

To convince these mighty executives to take time out of their busy three-hour workday to attend the show, volunteer to be their personal chauffeur to and from the conference center and to all the cigar and Cognac bars in town at night. No senior managers worth their toupee or makeup (or both) would turn down such a wonderful opportunity to fully assert their dominance over a middle manager.

As part of the deal, require that the senior manager goes to at least one conference session on forecasting and scheduling, one on determining feasible service levels, and one that explains that agents should be paid more than what the company spends on Perrier for the boardroom.

Commonly Confused Call Center Terms

The call center industry has evolved rapidly, which has resulted in numerous growing pains (and even a few call centers with 11 toes).

One of the most daunting aspects of this rampant growth, particularly for new managers and those who fake competence, is the veritable encyclopedia of call center terms that quickly spring up. Adding to the challenge is the fact that many of these terms sound alike but have completely different meanings.

For instance, while everybody knows that "talk time" is a metric that measures the time agents spend with a caller during a transaction; not everybody knows that "talk rhyme" is a metric that measures agents' ability to speak in poetic verse to distract angry customers whose accounts have been accidentally deleted.

Here are some more commonly confused call center terms that you should know:

After-call work

Work that is necessitated by and immediately follows an inbound transaction.

After-call *jerk*

1) An involuntary bodily twitch suffered by agents who have just handled their 15th "bill complaint" call in a row. 2) The general term for any derogatory name that agents scream at "bill-complaint" customers after the call is completed.

Best in class

A benchmarking term used to identify organizations that outperform all others in a specified category.

Best *gin* class

A benchmarking term used to identify call center managers who outperform all others at conference cocktail receptions.

ha ha ha ha ha ha ha ha ha ha ha ha ha ha ha

Calls in queue
A real-time report that refers to the number of calls received by the ACD system but not yet connected to an agent.

Calls in *coup* (*d'etat*)
What calls in queue become after they go unanswered for more than 10 minutes and cause angry customers to attack your company with flaming torches.

Cost per call
Total costs (fixed and variable) divided by total calls for a given period of time.

Cost per *fall*
Total cost of replacing agents who faint from exhaustion during the call center's peak season.

Erlang C
A formula used for calculating staff in a queuing situation.

Erlang *Sea*
A term for the pool of liquid that a call center manager is often reduced to after asking senior management for additional staffing.

Middleware
Software that mediates between different types of hardware and software on a network so that they may function together.

Middle*wear*
Any belt or straplike device that managers wrap around an agent's waist and workstation chair to enhance adherence-to-schedule statistics.

Occupancy
The percentage of time agents handle calls vs. waiting for calls to arrive.

Double occupancy
A common practice at service bureaus where two agents are crammed

into an already confining workstation to help the agency maintain "world-class" service levels.

Real-time management

Making adjustments to staffing and thresholds in the systems and network in response to current queue conditions.

Real-*mime* management

Intricate coaching and training techniques required by managers who hire Marcel Marceau to work in their call center.

Screen pop—(traditional use)

A CTI capability whereby a caller's account information is automatically delivered to an agent's desktop at the time the call arrives.

Screen pop—*(new use)*

What runs down an agent's desktop after he throws a can of Coke at it upon hearing that he has to work another weekend shift.

Skills-based routing

An ACD capability that matches a caller's specific needs with the agent most qualified to handle the call.

Skills-based *pouting*

What most managers resort to after experiencing the pain and suffering involved with scheduling the right agents to handle callers' specific needs.

Unified messaging

Integrated systems that enhance call centers' ability to manage voice-mail, email, Web and fax messages.

Unified *massaging*

A team-based relaxation method whereby agents collectively try to pacify a stressed-out team member and convince him to come in off the ledge.

For a complete dictionary of commonly confused call center terms, tear out these pages and put it in a nice leather binder.

ha ha ha ha ha ha ha ha ha ha ha ha ha ha ha

Pain-Free Monitoring Without Medication

Call monitoring ranks among the top three sources of manager headaches in our industry, along with staffing/turnover issues and forgetting to duck when walking beneath low-hanging readerboards.

Monitoring agents' calls for quality assurance and coaching purposes sounds so simple in theory, but in practice, the process seems to trip up many call center professionals. Managers and supervisors get entangled in the same questions time and time again: "What's the best monitoring method?" "How often should I evaluate calls?" "Did I just tape over my *Sinatra's Greatest Hits* cassette?"

Following are four effective practices that are guaranteed to enhance your call quality monitoring program year-round — unless, of course, they don't.

1. Get agent buy-in. Getting agents to embrace your monitoring program is essential for true quality success. Keeping agents from embracing supervisors' throats during feedback sessions is important, too.

The best way to achieve both is to involve agents in the development and maintenance of your monitoring program. Asking agents for input about how they would like to be monitored and what they feel qualifies as objective criteria are great ways to foster buy-in. They will not only feel valued and empowered when you frequently solicit their opinions, they will also feel that you aren't competent enough to make your own decisions, and thus will be less intimidated by you, further enhancing morale.

Another great way to get agents to accept your monitoring program is to stick sharp nails up through their seats and then promise to remove one nail for every call that you evaluate.

2. Create a standard, objective monitoring form. Once you've tricked agents into believing that monitoring is solely a means of quality improvement and not a way for you to feel superior, you need to develop a standard monitoring form that fosters consistent and objective evaluations.

Select specific criteria that are easily measurable and that elicit favorable actions: "Agent confirmed the caller's last name," "Agent used courteous phases," and "Agent blatantly lied about our return policy to secure the sale." Try to avoid more subjective criteria, such as "Agent was friendly" or "Agent was mean and probably abuses puppies in his free time."

To ensure that agents don't become complacent, you need to make it challenging for them to achieve a perfect monitoring score. On your form, include criteria such as "Agent guessed customer's full name," "Agent successfully completed call with mouth full of chunky peanut butter," and "Agent didn't blink."

3. Use a variety of monitoring methods. Familiarity breeds contempt, so it's important to mix up your monitoring methods (as well as to occasionally dress up like Carmen Miranda). Using a diverse mix of monitoring methods helps to keep your quality program fresh and each method offers its own unique benefits. For example, side-by-side monitoring lets you hear and see how agents handle calls; call-taping enables agents to later evaluate their own performance; peer monitoring reduces agent apprehension; and eavesdropping on agents' personal calls enables you to feel a little naughty.

4. Provide immediate, positive feedback. Even with initial buy-in from agents and a diverse mix of monitoring methods, your quality program will fail if you don't provide agents with proper feedback after an evaluated call. By "proper" I mean encouraging, focused feedback, preferably given while he or she is awake.

Use positive phrases to avoid sounding too critical. For example, if an agent fails to use the proper greeting during a call, don't make the common mistake of saying "Listen, punk, how do you expect to ever amount to anything if you can't even get a simple greeting right?" Instead, try phrasing your feedback thusly: "Wow, that's a lovely shirt. Too bad you totally blew the opening of that last call."

And remember, the feedback must be timely to have any measurable effect. Here are some signs that indicate you may be waiting too long to review calls with staff:

- Younger agents seem taller since the evaluated call.
- Older agents seem shorter since the evaluated call.
- The agent begins the feedback session by hugging you and showing you his or her children's college graduation pictures.
- You occasionally have to work your call comments into a eulogy.

Trust Me, Really

Some of my advice may seem a bit absurd, but only to those who read it. In any event, I promise that if you adopt these practices, you'll soon have more motivated agents, happier customers, fewer errors and rework, more motivated agents and happier customers.

Monitoring Misunderstood

Emerging Trends
You May Not Know About

If you read only the popular call center press, you're not getting the full story about what's happening — or about to happen — in this eccentric industry. You have to delve into a variety of alternative sources to uncover all the lies and hype affecting call centers. For example, to get the latest industry scoop, I regularly consult such lesser-known, radical publications as *The ACDissenter, Routing for Revolutionaries, Off with Their Headsets* and, of course, the business section of *USA Today.*

It was in these publications that I first heard of such unique trends as staff-sharing, e-sourcing and agent-bronzing. Here are just a few other emerging call center trends that you may not be aware of.

1. Agent retention via hypnosis. Considering how long agent attrition has been rampant among call centers, it's a wonder that it has taken managers this long to discover the wonderful benefits of intensive cerebral manipulation. To reduce turnover, more and more managers are secretly hiring hypnotists who convince agents that the call center is their destiny and that other companies skin their employees and eat them.

The key to successful hypnosis is luring agents into a relaxed, sleepy state. Managers can accomplish this several ways: mixing Nyquil with the break room coffee; serving big turkey dinners in the cafeteria; hanging posters of people yawning throughout the center; and — the most common method — continuing to pay agents their current wages.

2. Journalists handling customer email. One of the most innovative trends that's emerging in call centers is the use of professional newspaper journalists to respond to customer email. Today's managers realize that, just because their traditional agents provide stellar phone service, it doesn't mean that they're cut out to type their names without using "spell-check."

The handful of daring centers that have tested the use of journalists to handle email report numerous benefits, such as dramatic increases in email response times, higher accuracy and free subscriptions to local papers. In addition, journalists tend to write email responses that contain exciting "headlines" like "Bank Ignores Plea for Mercy — Credit Card Customer Riddled by Rate Increase."

However, it should be noted that using newspaper journalists has its drawbacks: They demand higher pay than traditional agents; they demand more liquor than traditional agents; and they may snoop around and break the story about your center's use of agent hypnosis.

3. Customers handling their own calls. For years, everyone in the call center industry has been talking about the importance of giving customers more control. Well, some call centers are finally doing something significant about it: They're hiring customers to handle their own calls. The philosophy behind this trend is that nobody knows a customer's needs and expectations quite like the customer (except perhaps the customer's mother and employees of the "Psychic Connection").

Hiring customers and training them how to answer their own product/service questions, how to cross-sell and upsell to themselves, and how to handle themselves when they become irate because of a shipping mix-up will enable call centers to achieve the ultimate in personalized service and customer satisfaction. The other benefit of hiring customers as agents is that measuring employee and customer attrition can be done in a single, easy step.

4. Vendors developing diabolical techno-glitches. Many people mistakenly believed that technology vendors were behind the Y2K bug in an effort to boost profits. While this was found to be untrue, the accusations did give many vendors ideas for the future. For example, several vendors have reportedly formed an alliance called THUD (Technology Havoc Under Development) whose sole objective is to concoct universal system bugs, create general hysteria about those bugs among call center professionals and induce a mad rush for system upgrades and replacements.

A couple of the bugs you'll soon be hearing about include:

- "Heartworm" — Set to occur on Valentine's day (February 14), the Heartworm virus is programmed to make call center standalone ACDs realize how solitary they are, causing them to literally fall apart.

- "VRU Talkin' to Me?" — Set to occur on Robert DeNiro's birthday (August 17), this debilitating bug will cause most call center VRUs to develop a thick New York accent and to greet callers with angry, intimidating messages like "You talkin' to me?" and "Shut ya freakin' trap!" and "Ya dead!"

Publisher's Note: We will continue to provide you with Greg's reports on such "lesser-known" industry trends as they progress, assuming the sanatorium administrator doesn't take away Greg's typewriter.

This ought to improve our 'adherence to schedule' statistics.

ha ha ha ha ha ha ha ha ha ha ha ha ha ha ha

ha ha ha ha ha ha ha ha ha ha ha ha ha ha ha

The Do's and Don'ts of Telecommuting

Introducing a work-at-home agent (a.k.a. "telecommuting") program at your call center can yield tremendous benefits. Well-implemented telecommuting programs enable you to enhance productivity and agent retention, reduce operating costs and remove agents with chronic bad breath from the call center without actually having to fire them.

But establishing and managing a successful work-at-home initiative isn't easy. It requires careful planning, clear communication and tremendous patience with hyperactive Cocker Spaniels that attack your ankles when you visit agents at home.

While there really is no clear-cut formula for implementing a successful work-at-home agent program, I have written this article as if there is so that I appear as competent as other industry experts.

Here are a few of my do's and don'ts to keep in mind when creating and/or maintaining a call center telecommuting program:

Do

Convince senior management of the financial merits of using work-at-home agents. Explain how, while setting up home agents does require an additional investment in equipment, the savings from increased agent retention alone will more than justify that investment, according to several studies that cost a ton of money and, thus, must be accurate.

Also explain how these studies have shown that telecommuting agents often generate more revenue than in-house agents because of fewer on-the-job distractions. If management doesn't buy the fact that agents won't be distracted at home, promise them that all telecommuters will have their televisions, stereos, refrigerators and neighbors removed at once.

Don't

Take agent selection lightly. Once you gain approval from upper management, it's time to focus on the most important element of any work-

73

at-home agent program: deciding which agents will be given the unique opportunity to handle valuable calls at home in their underwear.

Careful home agent selection demands an ample investment in time. Create a team of managers and supervisors who will interview all interested telecommuting candidates. Narrow your choices down to those agents who have demonstrated superior performance and attendance, who have proven they can work well independently, and who don't live in their cars.

Don't

Forget to draw up a standard contract for work-at-home agents. It's important to have a formal document that clearly communicates to telecommuters what's expected of them once they begin working from home.

For instance, if you don't want at-home agents running a small casino out of their basement during work hours, make sure you say so in the contract. The contract should also spell out such things as adherence requirements, remote monitoring practices, on-call requirements and limitations on the number of screeching cockatoos agents are permitted to have near their workstations.

Do

Take measures to avoid agent isolation. Even the most independent telecommuter needs occasional social interaction with co-workers to avoid alienation and elaborate conversations with pets. Invite work-at-home staff into the center to attend monthly meetings, office parties and agent floggings. In addition, occasionally visit each telecommuter at home to provide hands-on coaching and feedback. Schedule these visits during low-volume times to avoid service disruptions—or around 6 p.m. to enhance your chances of receiving a free home-cooked meal.

How do you know if your home agents are suffering from feelings of isolation? Look for the following classic, though often subtle, signs: 1) decreased productivity; 2) exorbitant talk times; 3) incessant cries of "Please don't leave me!" to supervisors at the end of home visits; and 4) home offices filled with life-sized cardboard figures of coworkers.

Do

I ever need to take a break! So that's it for now. If you have any questions about the benefits and drawbacks of telecommuting, or if you want to discuss why telecommuters have fewer distractions on the job, feel free to call me at my home office (800-555-SLAK)—I'm usually at my desk at 8:30, 10:20, 12:15; 2:00 and 4:07.

Telecommuters at Corporate Holiday Parties

ha ha ha ha ha ha ha ha ha ha ha ha ha ha ha

A Brief Guide to Progressive Agent Incentives and Recognition

Numerous studies have shown that agents who feel overstressed, underpaid and unappreciated treat customers poorly, make numerous errors and are three times more likely than happy agents to set a supervisor on fire. In fact, of the 15 incidents where call center supervisors caught fire last year, 14 were caused by agents with low morale (the 15th incident was the result of a vacationing supervisor who got careless during a volcano expedition).

Call centers without innovative incentives and recognition practices often incur astronomical turnover rates and poor customer loyalty. Yet few centers have implemented truly progressive practices that inspire agents to achieve organizational objectives and to forget the fact that they are chained to cubicles.

Here a few examples of what I believe are the most creative and promising motivational tactics around. (Note: Some of these ideas are still a bit unrefined. You may want to first test them out on lab mice or a select group of agents you particularly dislike.)

1. Executive suites for top performers. You can't expect agents to feel proud and continually meet the high demands placed on them if they continue to be shackled to cramped workstations in a warehouse environment. You need to show them that they are just as valuable to the company as the CEO. That's why I suggest building an octagonal-shaped call center where your top eight performers each get to work in a corner office.

Agents will knock themselves out on the phones to earn the right to occupy one of these "executive suites." To sweeten the pot and to provide agents with a real feeling of power, you can also give those who attain "agent executive" status a key to the executive washroom, permit them to speak to customers via speakerphone and give them the right to completely ignore the rest of the call center staff.

It's best to rotate top performers in and out of the executive suites on weekly or monthly basis. Longer stays may cause agents to start recommending staffing shortages and negotiating mergers.

2. Radical title change. Another great way to make agents feel important and valued is to change their job titles to something that commands more respect.

Instead of the bland "agent" or "rep," try something creative like "Headset Honcho," "Contact King," "Queue Queen" or the increasingly popular "The Artist Formerly Known as Operator."

You'd be amazed at how a radical title change can impact motivation and performance. For example, a catalog call center in Eau de Fromage, Wisconsin, recently conducted a revealing experiment where it separated agents into three groups, giving the agents in each group a different title: 1) "Agent"; 2) "Customer Specialist"; and 3) "Service Overlord."

The results were remarkable: The "Agent" group achieved mediocre service levels, reported high turnover and set two supervisors on fire. The "Customer Specialist" group faired better—achieving average service levels with a moderate rate of turnover and setting only one supervisor on fire. In comparison, the "Service Overlord" group exceeded all service level objectives, had zero turnover and quickly extinguished the three supervisor fires.

3. Spell-based pay program. Two unfortunate call center facts:
- Most agent salaries wouldn't even pay for one of the CEO's golf clubs; and
- Most agents can't even spell "CEO" when writing customer email.

One of the best ways to enhance agent wages (and retention rates) while, at the same time, improving your center's email response quality is to introduce a formal "spell-based pay" program.

Here's how it works: For every correctly spelled word in an agent's email response, you pay them 5 cents—or 1 cent if you manage a service bureau. Not only will such a program enable agents to earn some much-needed additional money and inspire them to improve, it will greatly reduce the chances of your call center being paid a visit by editors from Merriam-Webster.

The only real drawback of a spell-based pay program is that as agents' writing improves, they may earn enough money to buy a newspaper and find other job opportunities in the area.

Publisher's Note: If you would like to order a complete listing of Greg's ideas on developing progressive agent incentives and recognition practices, send a note telling him to come up with more—there's a reason why this is a "brief" guide.

Rep Empowerment Gone Awry

How to Reach the Publisher

We would love to hear from you! How could this book be improved? No comments are off limits! You can reach us at:

Mailing Address:	Call Center Press, a division of ICMI, Inc.
	P.O. Box 6177
	Annapolis, MD 21401
Telephone:	410-267-0700, 800-672-6177
Fax:	410-267-0962
Email:	icmi@incoming.com
Web site:	www.incoming.com

About Incoming Calls Management Institute

and Call Center Press, a division of ICMI, Inc.

Incoming Calls Management Institute (ICMI) offers the most comprehensive training programs and educational resources available for call center management professionals. Established in 1985 and the first to offer training on call center management, ICMI is a global leader in call center management training, publications and consulting.

ICMI's focus is helping individuals and organizations understand the dynamics of call center management in order to improve operational performance and achieve business results. ICMI provides high-caliber education and consulting to organizations ranging from small, start-up firms to national governments to multinational corporations.

Call Center Press, a division of ICMI, publishes the authoritative journal *Call Center Management Review* and the popular "how-to" book for call center managers, *Call Center Management On Fast Forward.*

A recognized pioneer in the field of call center management, ICMI is independent and not associated with, owned by or subsidized by any industry supplier.

Visit www.incoming.com for more information on ICMI, industry resources, research and links, and to join a network of call center management professionals.

CONTACT INFORMATION:

Mailing Address: P.O. Box 6177
Annapolis, MD 21401
Telephone: 410-267-0700, 800-672-6177
Email: icmi@incoming.com
Web site: www.incoming.com (ICMI)

ha ha ha ha ha ha ha ha ha ha ha ha ha ha ha

Author, Author!

Greg Levin is the former editor of *Call Center Management Review.* Greg is a regular contributor to the publication, and is currently a freelance writer based in Spain.

Fun Stuff Order Form

QTY.	ITEM	PRICE
	Call Center Humor: The Best of Call Center Management Review, Volume 3 (order copies for everyone you know)–$9.95 each* *Multiple Publication Sales Discount	
	Call Center Humor: Volume 1 (published as In Your Ear: A Compendium of Call Center Satire)–$9.95 each* *Multiple Publication Sales Discount	
	Call Center Humor: Volume 2 (published as In Your Ear: A Compendium of Call Center Satire)–$9.95 each* *Multiple Publication Sales Discount	
	The Call Centertainment Book 2 pages, soft-bound, filled with call center-related crossword puzzles, word searches, true/false quizzes and word scrambles–$8.95	
	Call Center Humor Mouse Pads better than cutting out the pages of this book–$6.95 circle selection(s): "Monitoring Misunderstood" (see p. 67); "Call Center: The Movie" (see p. 29); "Rep Empowerment Gone Awry" (see p. 79)	
	Call Center Travel Coffee Mug features "Prehistoric VRU" cartoon (see p. 35) –4 oz. auto mug with double wall construction and spill-resistant thumb slide lid provides significant heat and cold retention, not to mention staff retention–$3.95	
	Call Center Humor T-Shirts –100% heavy cotton short sleeve tee features cartoon on the back–$12.95 *(Please call or order online to select size, color, and cartoon featured)*	

Serious Stuff Order Form

QTY.	ITEM	PRICE
	Call Center Management On Fast Forward Book–281 pages, paperback, more than 100 charts and graphs $34.95 each* *Multiple Publication Sales Discount	
	Call Center Management On Fast Forward Book on Tape $49.95 each	
	Call Center Management Review monthly 20-page newsletter–$287 (1-year subscription)	
	Call Center Management Review ONLINE access the current issue and the key-word searchable article archives on our Web site–$287 (1-year subscription)	
	Call Center Forecasting and Scheduling: The Best of Call Center Management Review – 104 pages, paperback, more than 35 charts and graphs–$16.95 each* *Multiple Publication Sales Discount	
	*CD-ROM Tools for Incoming Call Center Managers–$49.00 each***	

*11-20 Copies (10% off) • 21-50 Copies (20% off) • 50+ Copies (30% off)

**CD-ROM includes software with the Erlang C and Erlang B formulas to calculate staff, occupancy, trunk load, service level, average speed of answer and calls in queue, as well as other software tools.

❏ Yes, please send me a free issue of *Call Center Management Review* and information on other publications and seminars.

Please ship my order and/or information to:

Name _____

Title _____

Industry _____

Company _____

Address _____

City_____State _____Postal Code ____

Telephone (   ) _____

Fax (   ) _____

Email_____

Method of Payment (Check one)

❏ Check enclosed (Make payable to ICMI Inc.; U.S. Dollars only)

❏ Charge to: ❏ American Express   ❏ MasterCard   ❏ Visa

   Account No. _____

   Expiration Date_____

   Name on Card _____

      Fax order to: 410-267-0962
         call us at: 800-672-6177 (410-267-0700)
    order online at: www.incoming.com
  or mail order to: ICMI Inc.
                   P.O. Box 6177, Annapolis, MD 21401

Fun Stuff Order Form

QTY.	ITEM	PRICE
	*Call Center Humor: The Best of Call Center Management Review, Volume 3 (*order copies for everyone you know*)–$9.95 each** *Multiple Publication Sales Discount	
	Call Center Humor: Volume 1 (published as In Your Ear: A Compendium of Call Center Satire)–$9.95 each* *Multiple Publication Sales Discount	
	Call Center Humor: Volume 2 (published as In Your Ear: A Compendium of Call Center Satire)–$9.95 each* *Multiple Publication Sales Discount	
	The Call Centertainment Book 2 pages, soft-bound, filled with call center-related crossword puzzles, word searches, true/false quizzes and word scrambles–$8.95	
	Call Center Humor Mouse Pads better than cutting out the pages of this book–$6.95 circle selection(s): "Monitoring Misunderstood" (see p. 67); "Call Center: The Movie" (see p. 29); "Rep Empowerment Gone Awry" (see p. 79)	
	Call Center Travel Coffee Mug features "Prehistoric VRU" cartoon (see p. 35) –4 oz. auto mug with double wall construction and spill-resistant thumb slide lid provides significant heat and cold retention, not to mention staff retention–$3.95	
	Call Center Humor T-Shirts –100% heavy cotton short sleeve tee features cartoon on the back–$12.95 *(Please call or order online to select size, color, and cartoon featured)*	

Serious Stuff Order Form

QTY.	ITEM	PRICE
	Call Center Management On Fast Forward Book–281 pages, paperback, more than 100 charts and graphs $34.95 each* *Multiple Publication Sales Discount	
	Call Center Management On Fast Forward Book on Tape $49.95 each	
	Call Center Management Review *monthly 20-page newsletter–$287 (1-year subscription)*	
	Call Center Management Review ONLINE access the current issue and the key-word searchable article archives on our Web site–$287 (1-year subscription)	
	Call Center Forecasting and Scheduling: The Best of Call Center Management Review – 104 pages, paperback, more than 35 charts and graphs–$16.95 each* *Multiple Publication Sales Discount	
	CD-ROM Tools for Incoming Call Center Managers–$49.00 each**	

*11-20 Copies (10% off) • 21-50 Copies (20% off) • 50+ Copies (30% off)

**CD-ROM includes software with the Erlang C and Erlang B formulas to calculate staff, occupancy, trunk load, service level, average speed of answer and calls in queue, as well as other software tools.

❏ Yes, please send me a free issue of *Call Center Management Review* and information on other publications and seminars.

Please ship my order and/or information to:

Name _____

Title _____

Industry _____

Company _____

Address _____

City_____State _____Postal Code ____

Telephone (   ) _____

Fax (   ) _____

Email_____

Method of Payment (Check one)

❏ Check enclosed (Make payable to ICMI Inc.; U.S. Dollars only)

❏ Charge to: ❏ American Express   ❏ MasterCard   ❏ Visa

   Account No. _____

   Expiration Date_____

   Name on Card _____

        Fax order to: 410-267-0962
          call us at: 800-672-6177 (410-267-0700)
      order online at: www.incoming.com
      or mail order to: ICMI Inc.
                        P.O. Box 6177, Annapolis, MD 21401